ANIMAL EMOTIONS

WHEN

ELEPHANTS CRY

HEATHER MOORE NIVER

Enslow Publishing

101 W. 23rd Street
Suite 240
New York, NY 10011
USA

enslow.com

WORDS TO KNOW

anthropomorphizing Giving human features to animals.

emotion A strong feeling.

grieve To feel sadness, usually because of a death.

herd A big group of animals that live together.

matriarch The female that is in charge of a herd or group.

mourn To feel deep sadness, usually for a death.

physical Related to the body.

recognize To know something or someone based on a previous meeting.

veterinarian A doctor for animals.

CONTENTS

CHAPTER ONE

GREAT BIG TEARS

In 2014, an elephant from India made news headlines across the world. The elephant's name was Raju, and he was 50 years old. Raju was probably captured from the wild when he was still a baby. He may have been forced to work for around 27 different humans throughout his life. Many of his owners treated him badly. They made him wear chains around his legs all day and all night. Some chains had painful, sharp spikes. They made it hard for him to walk. Some of his

A Crying Baby

In Budapest, Hungary, a baby elephant was seen climbing onto the back of its mother after she died. When the mother's body was taken away, the baby cried tears.

Much like Raju, some elephants in India are chained with sharp spikes. Spending hours in these chains causes great pain and injures their legs.

Elephants seem to feel emotions, or strong feelings, like happiness, just like humans do.

owners hit him. Sometimes he was not given enough food and water.

In early July of that year, Raju's life changed. A group of wildlife workers rescued him. The workers and **veterinarians** brought him fruit and talked nicely to him. Raju's reaction surprised everyone. Tears streamed down his face. It seemed like the rescued elephant was crying tears of happiness! Today Raju is living happily and safely in the care of people who treat him well.

Human beings have many strong feelings, or emotions. We might feel **emotions** like being happy, sad, angry, or scared. But all kinds of animals seem to have feelings, too. Elephants seem to feel emotions such as happiness, anger, kindness, love, and sadness, too. Elephants, one of the largest animals on the planet, have even been known to shed great big tears! But why do elephants really cry?

> ## Fact
>
> A healthy elephant of Raju's height and age should weigh about 5 tons (4,500–4,800 kilograms).

CHAPTER TWO

WHY WE CRY

We usually think of crying when we see tears. But tears can occur for other reasons. Liquid drips from eyeballs in the form of tears. Tears help keep the eyes wet and healthy.

Some scientists wonder if tears are simply a **physical** reaction. They say that shedding tears is the definition of crying. If that is true, then almost all mammals cry. This is especially true if they live on land. They all need tears to keep their eyes wet.

Crying Chimp

Back in the 1870s, two chimpanzees lived together. When one of them died, the living chimp cried loudly and moaned. He seemed to be **mourning**! His keeper said he had never heard the chimpanzee make a noise like that. The chimp cried all day.

We know that humans cry for some other reasons, too. We sometimes cry as a way to show emotions and feelings like happiness, sadness, and anger.

Scientists cannot be sure whether or not animals like elephants are crying because of an emotion. Humans cry to show their feelings. But it's harder to know for sure why elephants and other animals cry. We cannot communicate with them, so elephants and other animals cannot tell us why they cry.

Some scientists think that elephants

Tears help keep your eyes wet. Other times, humans cry tears when they are sad, angry, or even happy.

By watching how they act, we might learn some clues about why animals like elephants cry.

might cry because of emotion like we do. Although they cannot communicate with the animals with language, they

can observe, or watch, them to see how they behave. Raju is just one example. Remember, many people believe that this elephant cried with happiness when he was rescued.

Another example of an elephant crying is a baby named Zhuang Zhuang in China. After his birth, his mother tried to step on him. She seemed to try to injure her son. Zhuang Zhuang huddled under a blanket and cried great big tears for hours afterward. Some experts think that Zhuang Zhuang needed the contact of his mother. All babies automatically want the touch of their mothers right after they are born. When Zhuang Zhuang could not connect with his mother, he may have felt a terrible loss and cried.

CHAPTER THREE

SOUND OF SADNESS

Elephants don't see very well. So they depend on their other senses to get by. Elephants use smell, touch, and sound to help **recognize** one another. Elephants use sound especially to identify other elephants. Scientists

think that these big beasts might be able to recognize the sounds or voices of 100 other elephants.

Elephants can even communicate with other elephants up to 50 miles (about 80 kilometers) away! Elephants have very sensitive trunks and feet. They can feel tiny movements, or vibrations, in the ground.

Elephants feel sound and movement with their trunks and feet. These are ways they identify one another and communicate.

Elephants can make loud trumpet-like sounds with their trunks. Sounds help them show how they feel.

Sad Parrot

A parrot named Tiko showed grief when his owner died. Tiko did not cry tears. Instead, he howled all night long. He had never made this noise before. He had also never made so much as a peep at night before.

Sound is also a way for elephants to communicate with one another. It helps them share how they are feeling with their friends and family. Some sounds that elephants make to show sadness can include shouting, sobbing, or crying. Elephants have been seen making these sad sounds when one member of their herd dies. Just like elephants, humans also sometimes cry or moan when someone close to them dies.

Elephants use sounds for other emotions, too. When they are happy, elephants use their trunks to make a loud sound like a horn. When a new baby elephant is born, the females of the herd make loud noises, too.

Tears do not always mean someone or something is crying. Human beings cry as soon as they are born. But they do not cry with tears until several months later. Until then, their crying is only made up of sounds.

CHAPTER FOUR

OTHER SIGNS OF SADNESS

The fact that elephants have other very strong senses might be important. A tiny stream of tears is hard to see on a huge elephant. (Remember, they do not have very good eyesight!) Their senses of smell or hearing might be a lot more important in showing sadness. Perhaps their way of crying is different than how humans cry.

Do They Hear What We Hear?

Scientists are just learning how elephants communicate using sound and movement. But they do know that elephants can hear sounds that humans cannot.

This elephant seems to recognize the bones of a family member. Elephants touch and smell only the bones of an elephant they knew.

Elephants use their sense of smell as they **grieve**. When an elephant passes by an area where a friend or family member died, it stops. It touches and smells only the bones of the elephant it recognizes.

Sometimes elephants taste the bones of a herd member. They might also click them together.

Another way to measure animal emotions is to look at body language, or how it acts in certain events. For example, some scientists think that the way elephants rock and move when they find the bones of a herd member is a way of grieving. Rocking together might be a way they express their grief. When another elephant is dying, they might also make noise, go off to be alone, and stop eating or sleeping. These are all actions humans take when they mourn, too. Elephants have been seen making these movements

Elephants sometimes rock together when a member of their herd dies.

many times. The repetition helps convince scientists that elephants probably feel sadness, too.

Elephants also use body language to express when they are happy. For example, they flap their ears when they meet up with another elephant they know.

When elephants realize one of their herd is upset, they hurry to help. They make soft noises and stroke the elephant's head. Sometimes they put their trunks over or in the upset elephant's mouth. This seems to be calming, like holding someone's hand when you're scared. It is also a sign of trust, because the other elephant could chomp down on his or her trunk!

CHAPTER FIVE

A LOT LIKE HUMANS?

Some scientists do not think that elephants (or any other animals, for that matter) have emotions at all. They believe that only human beings cry emotional tears. If an animal cries, its tears may only be a physical reaction.

Some scientists say that we should not think of animals as having the same qualities as we do. For

Changing Tears

Even the tears of human beings are different, depending on the person's emotions. The tears change based on the person's mood as he or she cries. Scientists are still learning about different kinds of human tears.

These elephants seem to be having fun together. But some scientists are not so sure that animals experience emotions.

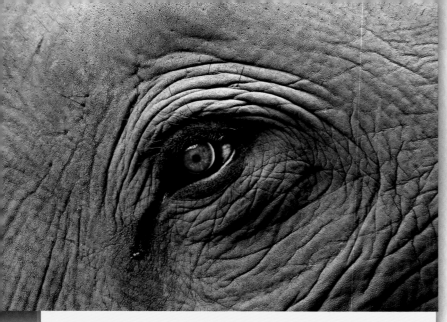

Many glands surround an elephant's eye.
These glands create tears and other liquids.

example, just because we cry when we are sad does not mean than an elephant does the same thing. It may be a long time before we know for sure what goes on in the minds of animals.

Not every human reacts the same way in every situation. For example, not everyone laughs at the same jokes. Not everyone cries at the same movies. So, we should not assume that animals react in the same ways as humans.

And of course, communicating with animals is a challenge. We do not speak the same language. Figuring out whether or not animals express emotions is extremely difficult.

If they are not sad, what is going on when elephants cry? Some scientists point out that elephants have a lot of **glands** around their eyes. Glands are organs in an animal's body that make a product and get rid of it. Elephants have many glands that make tears. But these tears are not the clear salty liquid, like human tears. They make other kinds of liquids too.

> ## Fact
> Giving human qualities to animals is called **anthropomorphizing**.

CHAPTER SIX

GREAT BIG GRIEF

If elephants do feel emotions, then grief seems to be one of the most powerful. When a family member dies, for example, elephants seem to mourn. An elephant mother in Kenya, Africa, saw her baby die. There had not been enough food to keep the baby alive. She tried to move it and lift it with her feet. The mother elephant stood over her baby's body for an hour after it died. Sometimes elephants will stand over the body of a dead family member for days.

Sad for the Sick or Dying

Elephants and dolphins carry their young when they are sick or dying. They might carry them for days. Scientists have never seen them carry their babies that are healthy and well.

When this young elephant died, its mother spent hours standing with her baby.

When elephants come across some elephant bones, they sometimes pick them up on their tusks. They might put the bones in their mouths, too. If there are bones belonging to more than one elephant mixed together, elephants can recognize which ones belong to their friends or family.

Elephants do something else that is curious when they discover the bones of another elephant they once knew.

They move the bones and hold them in their trunks. A **matriarch** elephant named Big Tuskless died of natural causes. A scientist was working at a camp nearby. She took one of the elephant's bones back to the camp to study it. Within a few days, Big Tuskless's herd came through camp. They walked straight to the matriarch's bone. They knew exactly which one was hers, even though there were dozens of other elephant bones there. Every member of the herd touched the bone and spent time with it. Then they all moved on. One elephant named Butch stayed behind for a while. Butch was Big Tuskless's son.

Elephants may recognize their family's bones even if they have been dead for many years.

This elephant mourns the death of his friend. Elephants find the bodies of their friends and families if they are moved.

Sometimes elephants explore human bones, too. But they leave the bones of most other animals alone.
 Sometimes scientists or hunters will move the whole body of an elephant, not just one bone. The elephant's herd will seek out the body. Each elephant

will pick up a bone and take it back to the place where the elephant died or was killed.

It may be a long time before we understand whether elephants cry when they are sad. But we do know that scientists will continue to study them and learn about their tears and emotions.

Books

Antill, Sara. *An Elephant's Life.* New York, NY: Powerkids Press, 2012.

McAneney, Caitie. *How Elephants and Other Animals Hear the Earth.* New York, NY: Powerkids Press, 2016.

Murray, Julie. *Elephants* (Big Buddy Books: African Animals). Minneapolis, MN: ABDO Publishers, 2012.

Websites

Elephant Lands
oregonzoo.org/discover/new-zoo/elephant-lands
See elephants at the Oregon Zoo, where they have created a natural home for them. Learn more about elephants with facts and photos.

National Geographic
video.nationalgeographic.com/video/elephant_african_mourning
National Geographic provides video of elephants grieving over the death of a family member.

Raju's Journey to Freedom—A Photo Journal
wildlifesos.org/blog/rajus-journey-to-freedom-a-photo-journal
Read all about Raju's story and see pictures of the rescued elephant.

INDEX

Published in 2018 by Enslow Publishing, LLC.
101 W. 23rd Street, Suite 240, New York, NY 10011

Library of Congress Cataloging-in-Publication Data

Names: Niver, Heather Moore, author.
Title: When elephants cry / Heather M. Moore Niver.
Description: New York, NY : Enslow Publishing LLC, 2018. | Series: Animal emotions | Includes bibliographical references and index. | Audience: Grades 3 to 5.
Identifiers: LCCN 2016057565 | ISBN 9780766086173 (library bound : alk. paper) | ISBN 9780766088603 (paperback : alk. paper) | ISBN 9780766088542 (6-pack : alk. paper)
Subjects: LCSH: Elephants—Psychology—Juvenile literature. | Grief in animals—Juvenile literature.
Classification: LCC QL737.P98 N58 2017 | DDC 599.6715/13—dc23
LC record available at https://lccn.loc
.gov/2016057565

Printed in the United States of America

To Our Readers: We have done our best to make sure all website addresses in this book were active and appropriate when we went to press. However, the author and the publisher have no control over and assume no liability for the material available on those websites or on any websites they may link to. Any comments or suggestions can be sent by email to customerservice@enslow.com.

Photo Credits: Cover, p. 1 Lara Zanarini/Shutterstock.com; pp. 4, 8, 12, 17, 22, 26, 29 FLPA/Alamy Stock Photo; p. 5 Martin Harvey/Corbis Documentary/Getty Images; p. 6 Anup Shah/DigitalVision/Getty Images; p. 9 guruXOX/Shutterstock.com; p. 10 ankitsiroya/iStock/Thinkstock; pp. 12–13 Roy Giles/Photographer's Choice RF/Getty Images; p. 14 yuda chen/Shutterstock.com; p. 18 Images of Africa Photobank/Alamy Stock Photo; p. 20 Anup Shah/Minden Pictures/Getty Images; p. 23 pjmalsbury/E+/Getty Images; p. 24 Jiri Foltyn/Shutterstock.com; p. 27 FRIEDRICHSMEIER/Alamy Stock Photo; interior pages background image De Space Studio/Shutterstock.com.